THE
GLOW IN THE DARK
BOOK OF
SPACE

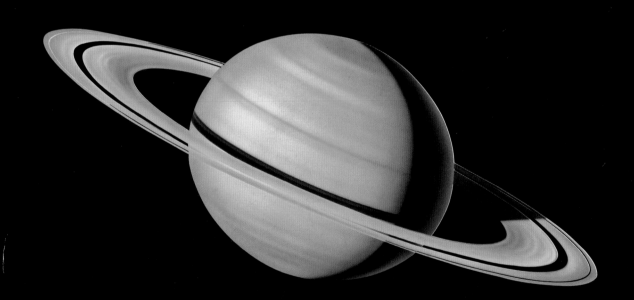

This edition published in 2013 by Frances Lincoln Children's Books,
4 Torriano Mews, Torriano Avenue, London NW5 2RZ
www.franceslincoln.com

Created and produced by Nicholas Harris and Claire Aston,
Orpheus Books Limited

Illustrated by Sebastian Quigley (Linden Artists)

Consultant: David Hawksett, Organiser of the UK Planetary Forum

Copyright © 2001 Orpheus Books Limited

First published in 2001 by Orpheus Books Limited

British Library Cataloguing in Publication Data available on request

ISBN 978-1-84780-417-4

Printed in China

7 9 8

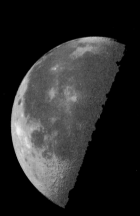

THE GLOW IN THE DARK BOOK OF

SPACE

Nicholas Harris

illustrated by
Sebastian Quigley

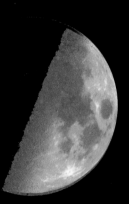

F

FRANCES LINCOLN
CHILDREN'S BOOKS

Meteors

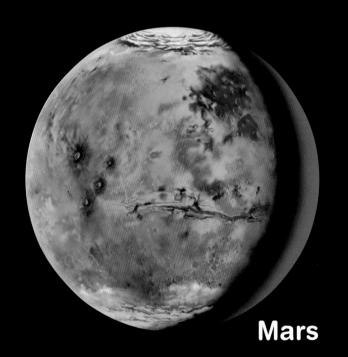

Mars

CONTENTS

WE THINK of space as the vast, dark expanse beyond our own planet Earth. The Sun's light fills the sky by day, of course, but at night other objects in space become visible: stars, the Milky Way, the Moon, shooting stars, and so on. We can see these objects because they glow, either with their own light, or with light reflected from the Sun. This book also shows objects in space that glow. For the pages with special glow-in-the-dark text and illustrations, look for the pink corner squares. Hold the book open at any one of these pages under a light for twenty seconds or so, then turn out the light. Have fun!

Milky
Way
Galaxy

ABOUT THIS BOOK

Planet

Comet

Moon

LOOK UP at the sky on a clear night. What is the brightest thing you can see? On many nights it will be the Moon. It looks so large and bright

because it is our nearest neighbour in space.

Stars may look tiny, but in fact they are all gigantic, thousands of times the size of Earth!

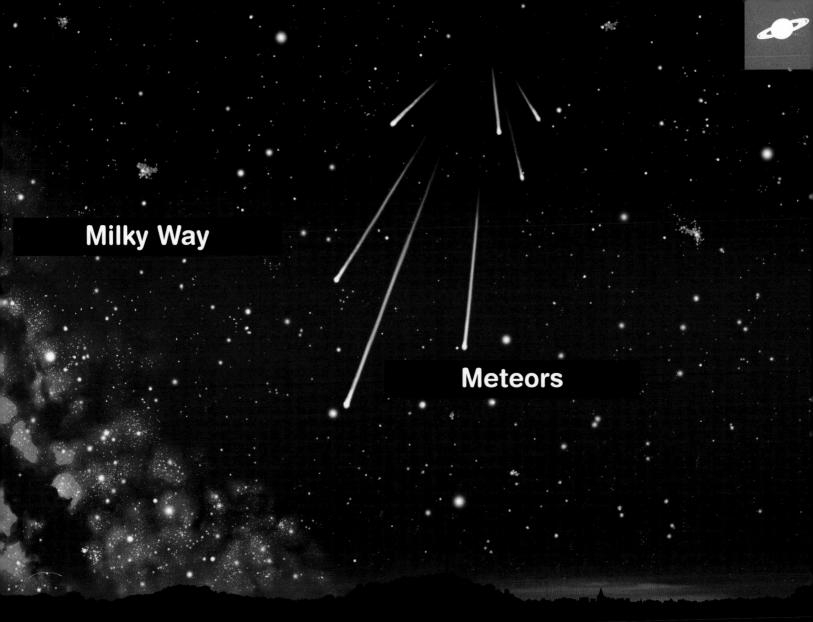

Milky Way

Meteors

All the stars we can see belong to the Milky Way Galaxy. From Earth, our view of one of the Galaxy's spiral arms looks like a misty band across the heavens, the "milky way" from which the Galaxy takes its name.

Sometimes, you may be able to catch sight of a comet hanging in the sky. Look out, too, for meteors or "shooting stars", split-second streaks of light. They are tiny fragments burning up high above Earth.

THE SUN is one of billions of stars that make up the Galaxy. Like all stars, it is a giant, spinning ball of very hot gas. It produces massive amounts of energy at its core.

The surface of the Sun bubbles and spits like water boiling in a pan. Huge flares and arches of glowing gas sometimes burst into space. Sunspots, dark, cooler areas, appear on the Sun's surface from time to time.

Arch

Jupiter
(to scale)

Earth
(to scale)

Flare

THE SUN

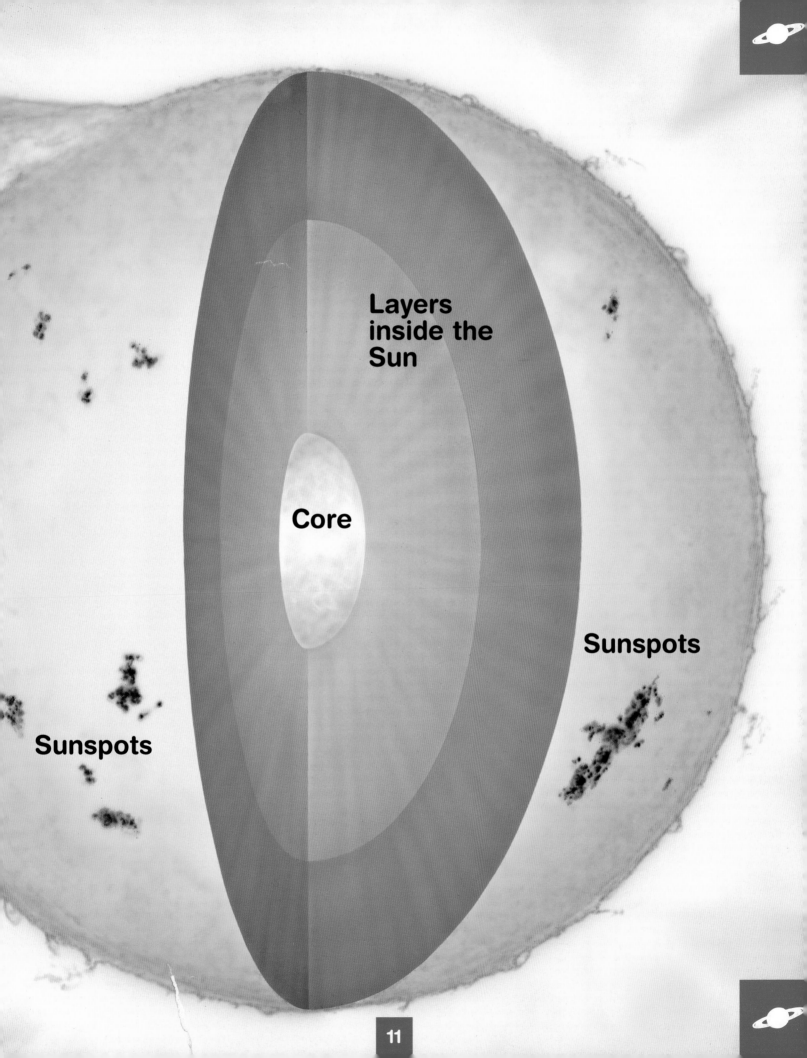

THIS IS what the Milky Way Galaxy would look like if we zoomed out into space and looked back down at it. It is a gigantic mass of stars. The swirling pattern the stars make is called a spiral. The Galaxy has a bulge at its centre. Our Sun is just one of the billions of stars in the Milky Way Galaxy. It is found on one of the spiral "arms", just over halfway out from the centre.

OUR GALAXY, A SPIRAL OF STARS

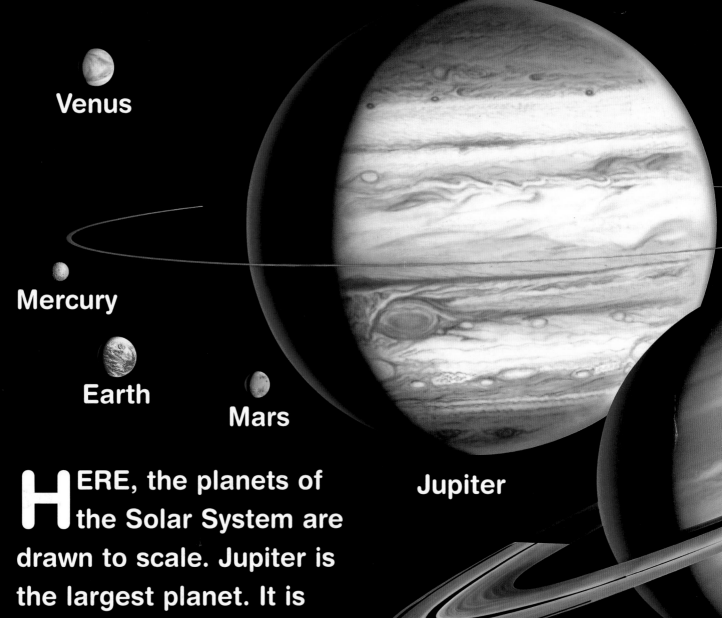

Venus

Mercury

Earth

Mars

Jupiter

HERE, the planets of the Solar System are drawn to scale. Jupiter is the largest planet. It is more massive than all the others combined.

The four inner planets are Mercury, Venus, Earth and Mars. They are mostly made of rock.

Sun
Mercury
Venus
Earth
Mars

Asteroids

Jupiter

Saturn

Uranus

Saturn

Neptune

Pluto

Much larger than the inner planets are the four outer planets, the "gas giants" Jupiter, Saturn, Uranus and Neptune. They are mostly made of gas. Pluto is the odd one out. Called a dwarf planet, it is made of ice and rock.

The diagram below, also drawn to scale, shows the distance each planet lies from the Sun.

THE PLANETS TO SCALE

Uranus

Neptune

THE SOLAR SYSTEM

THE SOLAR SYSTEM consists of the Sun, its family of planets and their moons, comets, asteroids, meteoroids and vast amounts of gas.

All these objects, large or small, travel around, or orbit, the Sun.

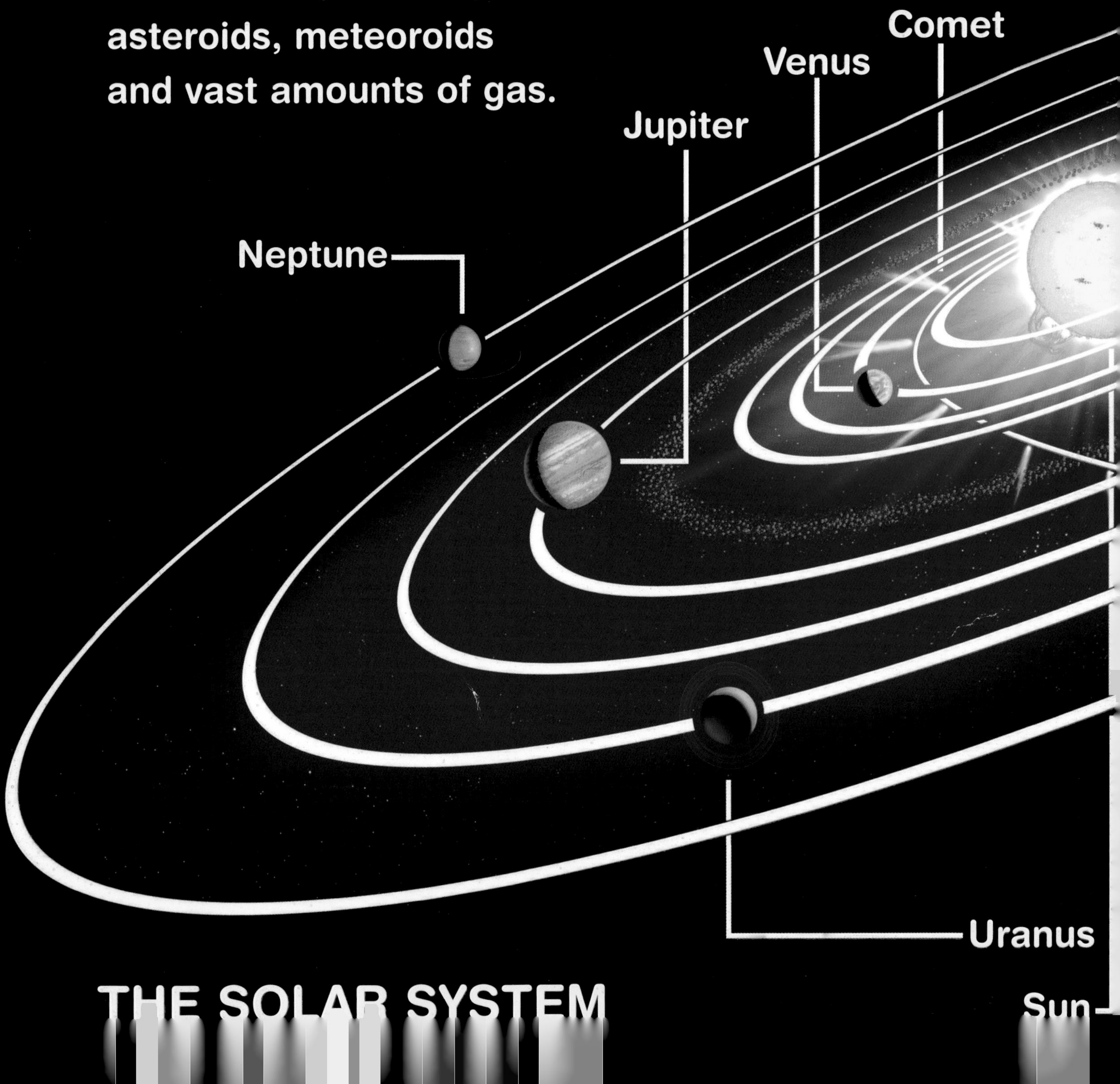

Comet

Venus

Jupiter

Neptune

Uranus

Sun

THE SOLAR SYSTEM

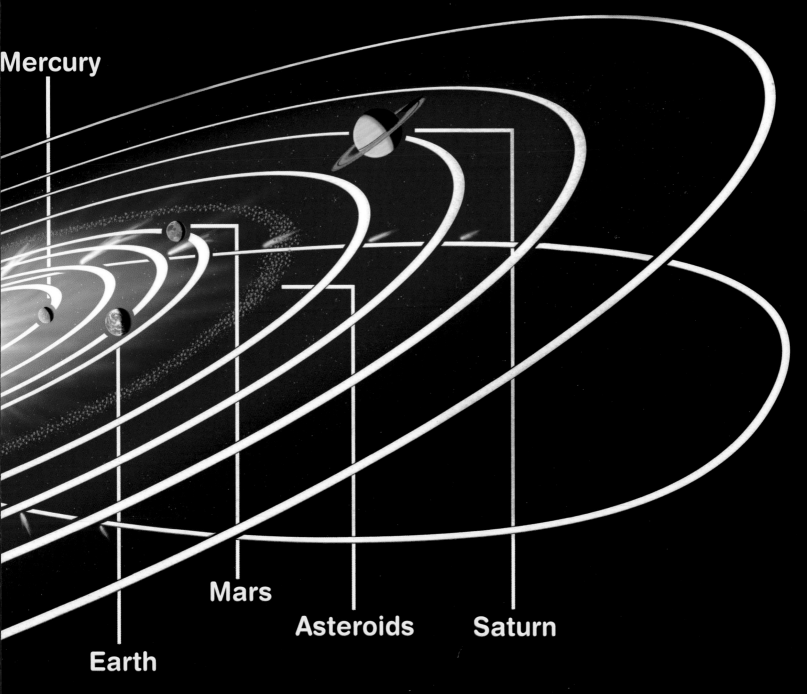

Mercury

Mars

Earth

Asteroids

Saturn

The planets orbit the Sun in the same direction (anticlockwise on the illustration) and on roughly the same plane.

Their orbits are not circular but oval-shaped. Many comets loop in towards the Sun from distant parts of the Solar System.

MERCURY is the nearest planet to the Sun. During the day it is extremely hot. But at night it is bitterly cold.

VENUS is covered in thick clouds of deadly acid. On its surface, the temperature is hot enough to melt lead.

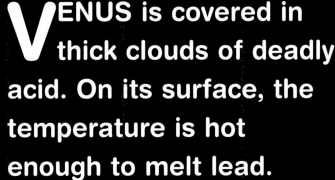

EARTH is the only planet to have liquid water, vital for any life to exist. The atmosphere protects us from the Sun's harmful rays.

THE INNER PLANETS

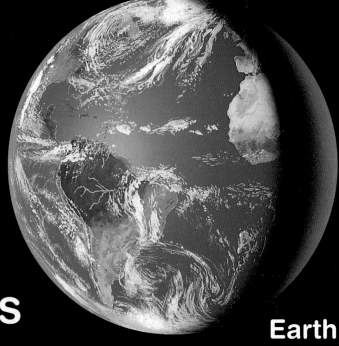

Earth

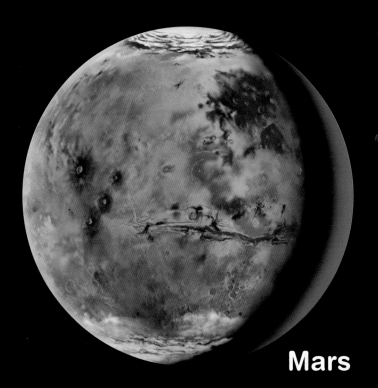

Mars

MARS is the "Red Planet", so-called

because of the colour of the dust that blankets its surface. Now completely barren, Mars may once have had running water. Some scientists think that there could have been life on Mars in the past. The only water on the Martian surface today is frozen at the polar icecaps.

Asteroids

ASTEROIDS are small blocks of rock and

metal. Most are found in a belt between Mars and Jupiter. Meteoroids, fragments of asteroids, sometimes come near Earth. Comets are lumps of dust and rock frozen together. Long tails of gas and dust are swept back by the Sun's rays.

Comet

THE MOON is a ball of rock that orbits the Earth. All the planets, except for Mercury and Venus, have moons. Our Moon is a barren world pitted with craters. These have been blasted out by rocks crashing down from space, called meteorites. There is no atmosphere on the Moon.

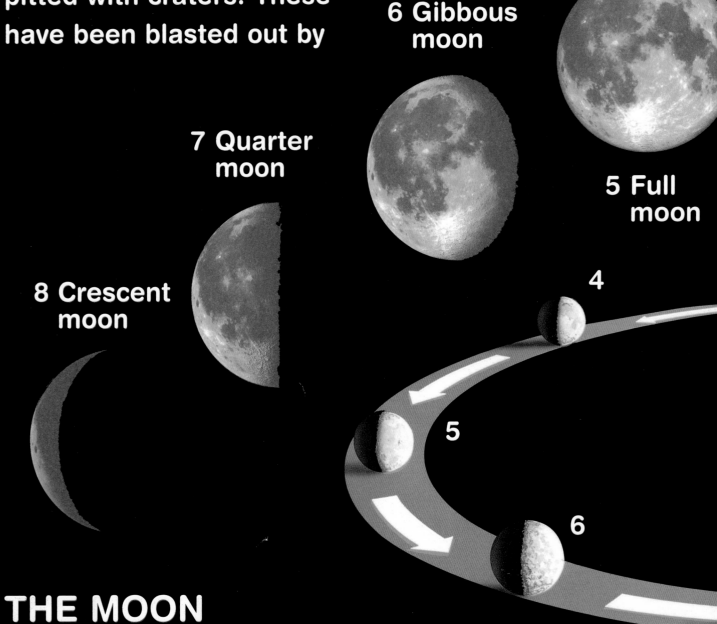

6 Gibbous moon

7 Quarter moon

5 Full moon

8 Crescent moon

4

5

6

THE MOON

4 Gibbous moon

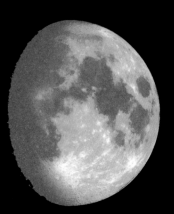

3 Quarter moon

2 Crescent moon

1 New moon

The shape of the Moon seems to change slightly each night *(above)*. This is because the same side always faces us as the Moon orbits Earth *(below)*. It is our view of the sunlit part that changes.

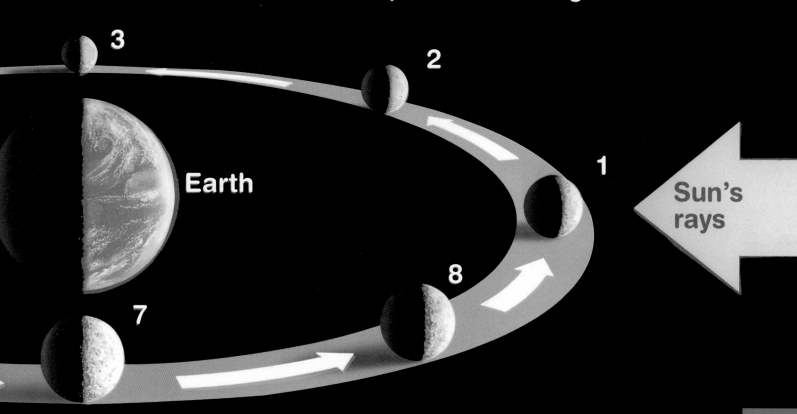

3

2

1

Earth

Sun's rays

8

7

Jupiter

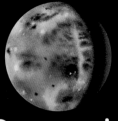

Ganymede

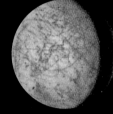

Callisto

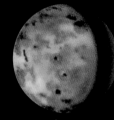

Io

Europa

JUPITER is large enough to contain 1300 Earths. Its patterns of red, yellow and white are produced by high-speed winds. The Great Red Spot is a giant storm. Jupiter's four largest moons *(above right)* are called the "Galileans".

SATURN is famous for its rings. They are made of billions of blocks of ice and rock. Saturn's largest moon, Titan, is the only moon in the Solar System to have a thick atmosphere.

Saturn

Titan

THE OUTER PLANETS

Triton

Uranus

Neptune

URANUS, the third gas giant, orbits the Sun lying almost on its side. The other planets orbit in a near-vertical position. Uranus has 11 faint rings and a family of 21 moons.

NEPTUNE is a bright blue globe with a few wispy clouds and, occasionally, dark spots. It has very faint rings. Neptune's largest moon, Triton, is the coldest world in the Solar System.

OTHER objects larger than Pluto have recently been discovered in the distant reaches of the Solar System. So Pluto is now called a "dwarf planet".

Pluto

Aquarius

Pisces

Cetus

Equuleus

Pegasus

Aries

Taurus

Delphinius

Andromeda

Perseus

Orion

Sagitta

Cassiopeia

Aquila

Cygnus

Cepheus

Lyra

Draco

Camelo-
pardalis

Auriga

Hercules

Ursa
Minor

Lynx

Ophiuchus

Corona
Borealis

Ursa Major

Monoceros

Serpens

Boötes

Gemini

Cancer

Canis
Minor

Coma
Berenices

Hydra

Virgo

Leo

YEARS AGO, people
saw patterns of stars   in the night sky. They
imagined their shapes to

CONSTELLATIONS

SOUTHERN HEMISPHERE

Pisces
Cetus
Aquarius
Eridanus
Sculptor
Phoenix
Grus
Fornax
Capricornus
Aquila
Lepus
Tucana
Sagittarius
Columba
Reticulum
Pavo
Dorado
Orion
Octans
Scorpius
Canis Major
Carina
Crux
Ophiuchus
Vela
Monoceros
Puppis
Centaurus
Lupus
Pyxis
Libra
Hydra
Corvus
Crater
Virgo
Sextans

ok like gods, heroes or
nimals from legends.
hese star patterns are
lled constellations.

Being able to recognize
constellations helps us to
find stars, galaxies and
other heavenly bodies.

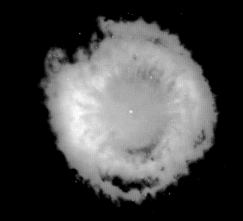

EVERYTHING that we know exists—stars, rocks, animals, people, air—all belong to the Universe. Nearly all matter is contained in galaxies *(below)*.

The Universe probably came into being about 15 billion years ago. There was a massive explosion called the Big Bang. All matter, energy, space—and time itself—were created in the Big Bang.

As the Universe expanded, the first stars were formed. Many, like our Sun, will shine on fo billions of years. But eventually they will swel into red giants before flaking away into space, A planetary nebula is all that will remain *(above).* A massive star will grow into a supergiant before exploding in a supernova (the remains of one are pictured *below).*

THE UNIVERSE

After a supernova, what is left of the old star may shrink to a tiny point. Around it, the force of gravity is so strong that nothing, not even light, can escape from it. We call these places black holes. Anything lying close to them, like the blue star shown in this illustration *(below)*, will be dragged in!

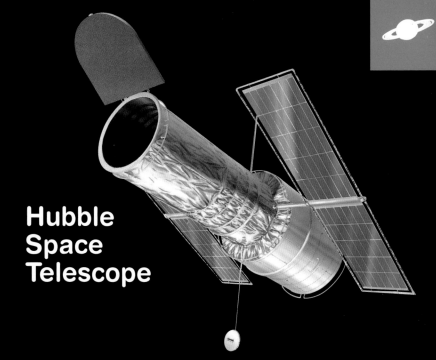

Hubble Space Telescope

Distances are so great in space that we have to use a special measure for them: a light year. This is the distance that light, which moves at about 300,000 kilometres per second, travels in one year. Proxima Centauri, the nearest star to us (apart from the Sun), is 4.2 light years away. The most distant objects we know are more than 13 billion light years away!

ASTEROID A small rocky body that orbits the Sun.

BIG BANG The explosion in which the Universe was created.

BLACK HOLE A region of space from which nothing, not even light, can escape.

COMET An lump of dust, ice and rock that orbits the Sun *(below)*. When it nears the Sun, long tails stream away from it.

USEFUL WORDS

CONSTELLATION A pattern of stars in the night sky.

CRATER A saucer-shaped feature found on the surface of some planets, moons and asteroids.

ECLIPSE The movement of a planet or moon in front of another, or in front of the Sun.

GALAXY An enormous cluster of stars, gas, dust and planets *(far right)*.

GRAVITY The force that attracts all objects to each other. Gravity is the force that keeps the planets orbiting the Sun.

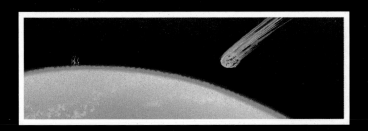

METEORITE A meteoroid that falls from space onto a planet or moon *(above)*.

METEOROID A piece of rock or dust that hurtles through the Solar System. When a meteoroid burns up close to Earth it is known as a **METEOR**.

ORBIT The circular or oval-shaped path followed by one object around another in space.

PLANET A world that orbits a star. It does not produce its own light.

SOLAR SYSTEM The Sun, the planets and their moons, comets, asteroids, meteoroids, dust and gas.

STAR A globe of gas (eg. the Sun) that produces energy inside its core.

SUPERNOVA The massive explosion of a supergiant star.

UNIVERSE All matter and space.

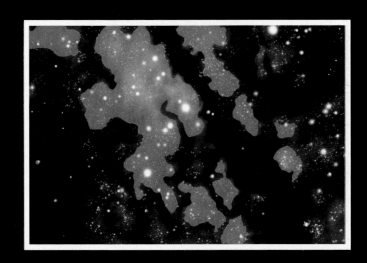

PLANET	DIAMETER	DAY measured in Earth days or hours	YEAR measured in Earth days or years	AVERAGE DISTANCE FROM SUN	SURFACE TEMPERATURE	MOONS
Mercury	4878 km	58.6 days	88 days	58 million km	-170 to +350°C	none
Venus	12,103 km	243 days	225 days	108 million km	490°C	none
Earth	12,756 km	23 hrs 56 min	365.26 days	149.6 million km	-70 to +55°C	1
Mars	6794 km	24.6 hours	687 days	228 million km	-137 to +26°C	2
Jupiter	142,884 km	9.8 hours	11.8 years	778 million km	-150°C	63
Saturn	120,536 km	10.2 hours	29.4 years	1427 million km	-180°C	60
Uranus	51,118 km	17.2 hours	84 years	2869 million km	-210°C	27
Neptune	50,538 km	16.1 hours	164.8 years	4497 million km	-220°C	13
Pluto	2324 km	6.4 days	248 years	5906 million km	-220°C	3